Reading Comprehension Workbook

Level 4

Series Designer
Philip J. Solimene

Editor
Dorothy M. Bogart

Reading Consultant
Sidney J. Rauch, Ed.D.
Professor of Reading and Education
Hofstra University, New York

EDCON

Story Authors
Roberta J. Harney
Esther Jewell
Miriam P. Kurinsky
Ronnie Levine Schindel
Malvina Vogel

Printed in U.S.A.
ISBN# 0-931334-52-7

CONTENTS

A Freedom Fighter in Two Worlds

Learn the Key Words

business (biz′ nis) someone's work
John is planning to go into his father's <u>business</u> when he gets out of school.

freedom (frē′ dəm) the state of being free
People in America have the <u>freedom</u> to say what they believe.

government (guv′ ərn mənt) the rulers of a country or state
The President is the head of the United States <u>government</u>.

officer (ôf′ ə sər)
1. a person in the army in charge of men
    Captain Glenn is an <u>officer</u> in the United States Army.
2. any policeman

prison (priz′ ən) a place where a law breaker is sent
When the thief was caught, he was sent to <u>prison</u> for five years.

soldier (sōl′ jər) someone serving in the army
Every <u>soldier</u> is trained in the use of guns.

Preview:

1. Read the title.
2. Look at the picture.
3. Read the first three paragraphs of the story.
4. Then answer the following question.

You learned from your preview that
_____ a. Haym Salomon came to America to fight.
_____ b. Haym Salomon came to America for freedom.
_____ c. Haym Salomon was a poor man.
_____ d. Haym Salomon could speak only Polish.

Turn to the Comprehension Check on page 4 for the right answer.

Now read the story.
Read to find out how Haym helped America win a war.

A Freedom Fighter In Two Worlds

Haym Salomon will have more trouble if those British soldiers know what he is saying to the Germans.

Back in the 1700s, Poland was one of the weakest countries in Europe. Other stronger countries kept trying to take over Poland's government. A small band of Polish men tried to keep their country free, but it was no use. Poland was taken over by a new government. The brave freedom fighters were forced to leave their country or be thrown into prison.

One of these freedom fighters was a young man named Haym Salomon. Haym decided to leave Poland and come to the New World, America. He believed that America was a land of freedom.

Haym came to New York and started his own business. It made him a very rich man. Haym made many friends among the people who had come here from all parts of Europe. He was able to speak to them because he knew many languages.

After Haym had been in America a few years, life began to change. Even though the American people had their freedom, they were still ruled by the English king. When the king tried to take away some of America's freedom, many Americans feared this would lead to war. Haym knew that if war came, he would fight for freedom in his new country just as he had done in his old country. But this time, he would win.

When war did come, New York was the first city the British soldiers took over. Many Americans left New York, but Haym stayed. He gave most of the money from his business to the American government. This helped pay the soldiers and buy guns for George Washington's army. He also joined a group of Americans who had been working secretly for many years to free their country from England. These men planned attacks on British soldiers and on British ships in New York Harbor.

When the British discovered what Haym was doing, they threw him into prison. But even in prison, Haym managed to continue his fight for freedom.

It happened this way. The British government needed extra soldiers to help fight the war in America. The king arranged to get them from Germany by paying the German government a lot of money.

When these German soldiers arrived in America, the British officers were faced with new troubles. None of the Germans spoke or understood English. And none of the British spoke or understood German. No one could give orders, and no one could understand them.

One British officer remembered that Haym spoke German. The officer offered to let Haym out of prison if Haym would help talk to the German soldiers. Haym thought about this for a while. He really didn't want to do anything that might help the British win the war. But, on the other hand, he had no way to help the Americans if he stayed in prison. Haym also realized that by helping the British, he could learn their war plans. Then, once he was free, he could tell those plans to George Washington. So Haym decided to help the British.

As the British officer was explaining to him what to tell the Germans, Haym suddenly thought of another plan. This new plan would put his life in danger, but if it worked, it would really help the Americans.

Haym stood up in front of a group of German soldiers and began to speak. The British officers watched him very closely, but they had no way of knowing what he was saying, for he was speaking in German. It was lucky for Haym that they didn't know!

For, instead of explaining the war plans to the Germans, Haym talked about America. He told them what it was like to live in a free country. He explained that America was fighting for its freedom. Then he offered the soldiers a chance to have their freedom, too. He showed them how they were taking chances with their lives while their government was getting all the money from England. Haym then promised the Germans that if they came over to the American side, George Washington would give them land for farms and homes. Then they would be free Americans, too.

Haym spoke so well that, at a later time, many German soldiers did run away from the British and join the American army. The British did not discover what Haym had done.

In a short time, they freed him from prison.

Haym returned to his home and to his business. He helped raise money from his friends for the American army. He gave most of his own money as well. He also continued his secret work with the freedom fighters.

America finally did win the war. Since that time, no country has ever tried to take away America's freedom. We can thank Haym Salomon and men like him for the freedom that every American enjoys today.

A Freedom Fighter in Two Worlds

COMPREHENSION CHECK

Choose the best answer.

1. Haym left Poland because
   ____a. he liked to travel to other countries.
   ____b. a new government came into power.
   ____c. he couldn't make any money there.
   ____d. George Washington told him to come to America.

2. Haym was able to make many friends in America because
   ____a. he spoke many languages.
   ____b. he was very rich.
   ____c. he knew them from Europe.
   ____d. he had fought for freedom in Poland.

3. War between America and England started because
   ____a. the English king wanted the Americans to return to England.
   ____b. both countries wanted to rule Poland.
   ____c. George Washington had a fight with the English king.
   ____d. the English king tried to take away America's freedom.

4. The money that Haym gave to the American government was used
   ____a. to buy soldiers from Germany.
   ____b. to build ships in New York Harbor.
   ____c. to pay the soldiers and buy guns.
   ____d. to send gifts to the English king.

5. The British government got extra soldiers for their army
   ____a. by using Americans who were in prison.
   ____b. by buying them from Germany.
   ____c. by taking over the Polish government.
   ____d. by forcing the Indians to fight for them.

6. When the German soldiers arrived in America, the British discovered that
   ____a. the Germans couldn't shoot British guns.
   ____b. the British soldiers didn't like German soldiers.
   ____c. none of the German soldiers understood English.
   ____d. the Germans really wanted the Americans to win.

7. If the British officers really knew what Haym was telling the German soldiers, they probably would have
   ____a. freed Haym right away.
   ____b. sent him back to prison.
   ____c. given him a medal.
   ____d. told George Washington about it.

8. Haym promised the German soldiers that George Washington would
   ____a. make them all officers in the American army.
   ____b. give them a lot of American money.
   ____c. give them land for farms and homes.
   ____d. let them go home to Germany.

9. Another name for this story could be
   ____a. "Freedom Fighters Today."
   ____b. "The Attack on New York Harbor."
   ____c. "German Soldiers in America."
   ____d. "One American's Courage."

10. This story is mainly about
    ____a. a freedom fighter who saved Poland from other countries.
    ____b. the training of soldiers in George Washington's army.
    ____c. a man who believed in freedom and fought for it twice.
    ____d. the tricks that the British used to win the war in America.

Check your answers with the key on page 53.

Idea starter: Other than soldiers, what people fight for freedom?

A Freedom Fighter in Two Worlds

VOCABULARY CHECK

Use the key words from the box to complete the sentences.

business	freedom	government	officer	prison	soldier

1. The _____ in charge of the Air Force Base was Captain Evans.

2. Mr. Marsh lowered the prices in his store hoping that _____ would get better.

3. The robber was sent to _____ for twenty years.

4. Joe's father is a _____ in the United States Army.

5. Our laws are made by the _____ in Washington, D.C.

6. Americans enjoy the _____ to speak out against their President if they believe he is wrong.

Check your answers with the key on page 55.

The Dance Of The Bees

Learn the Key Words

clover   (clō' vər)   a kind of flower-bearing plant
Bees like <u>clover</u> because it is rich in the sweet juice from which they make honey.

discovery   (dis kuv' ə rē)   the finding of something
The bee tells the hive about his <u>discovery</u> by doing a dance.

distance   (dis' təns)   the space between one place or thing and another
The bee tells the other bees the <u>distance</u> of the flowers from the hive.

language   (lang' gwij)   the words or other ways people and animals tell each other things
The <u>language</u> of the bees is made up of dance steps.

messenger   (mes' ən jər)   one who carries or brings a message
The honey bee is a good <u>messenger</u> for its hive.

swarm   (swôrm)
1. bees in a group
    A <u>swarm</u> of a thousand bees hung from the branch of a tree.
2. to get together in large numbers and move about, as a crowd might
    When the hive gets too crowded, thousands of bees <u>swarm</u> about the queen bee and leave the hive with her.

Preview:

1. Read the title.
2. Look at the picture.
3. Read the first paragraph of the story.
4. Then answer the following question.

Your preview told you
_____ a. that bees can growl.
_____ b. that bees always sting.
_____ c. that bees like to talk to people.
_____ d. that bees have a language of their own.

Turn to the Comprehension Check on page 9 for the right answer.

Now read the story.

Read to find out why bees "dance."

The Dance Of The Bees

One of these bees has just let the others know where there is a field of clover.

Someone you will read about: Karl von Frisch

Bzzzz . . . . . This sound tells you that a honey bee is around. To you, she seems to be saying, "Get out of my way or I'll sting you." But she uses quite another language to talk to her fellow bees.

Suppose the bee finds a patch of clover blossoms or some other sweet-smelling flowers. To a bee, a sweet-smelling flower means food. Flowers are rich in the juices (called *nectar*) that bees use to make honey.

The bee then flies back to the beehive quickly, for she can hardly wait to report what she has found. And when she gets back, she does a funny little "dance." Just by watching her, the other bees can tell where she discovered the clover. Soon, they are on their way to the spot themselves. After they collect sweet juices from it, they will bring it home. Later, it comes out as honey that they leave inside the hive in honeycombs.

Thousands of bees belong to every beehive, and each bee has a special job. Some bees do nothing but collect the sweet juices from flowers. Some guard the hive. Some keep it clean, and some make certain that the air inside does not grow too hot or too cold. Either way would not be healthy for the baby bees. There are also bees that do nothing but take care of the young.

The bee spends its life serving the needs of the beehive. Bees must work together very closely for life to go on, and for this reason they depend strongly on language. To be good messengers, they must know how to "talk" to one another.

About thirty years ago, someone discovered that bees have a language. Karl von

Frisch studied bees for many years. At last, it struck him that the funny little dances of the bees were words in their language. The bees were telling each other important things with their strange dance steps!

Can you imagine how excited Karl von Frisch was when he made his discovery!

Karl von Frisch saw that when a bee returns to the hive after finding something sweet, she does what looks like a wild dance. She dances in front of the other bees that have the job of gathering food. The different steps tell them the distance she had to travel to find the food and how the flowers smell. The other food-gathering bees join in the dance.

If the sweet food is only a short distance away, the dance that is done is called the "round dance." This is a dance in a circle, the bee going first in one direction and then making another circle, going in the other direction. When they know the prize is near, the other bees soon find it, flying about very quickly to the exact spot.

But if food blossoms are a mile or more away, the messenger bee does a different dance, called the "wagging dance." This dance has a lot more to say. In it, the bee runs about, in only part of a circle and then cutting across it. Then she does this again, wagging her body as she goes. If she dances very fast, she is saying that the distance is very far. The slower the dance, the closer is the field of clover or other flowers. The wonder of it all is that her dance tells the others exactly where to find the place. It shows them in which direction to fly and how to recognize the food by its smell.

When bees wish to move to a new home, certain bees have the job of going out alone to search for a place. When they return, each messenger does a dance to report to the hive what she has found. Each house hunter tries to prove that she has found the best place. Then there is a lot of "talk" back and forth. Finally, they decide on a new home. Karl von Frisch found that a lot of excitement goes on while the matter is being talked over.

There is another way that bees move to a new home. Thousands of honey bees leave, taking a queen with them. This group is called a "swarm." Where the queen lands, the swarm forms around her, hanging together like some great wagging beard. Karl von Frisch called this the "swarming dance."

Another amazing thing is that bees from different countries do not speak exactly alike. People from New York do not talk exactly like people from Texas, so why should bees everywhere have the same way of talking?

The Dance Of The Bees

COMPREHENSION CHECK

Preview answer:

d. that bees have a language of their own.

Choose the best answer.

1. When a bee comes upon a patch of sweet clover, she
   ____a. will sit on it to smell it.
   ____b. takes juices from it back to the hive.
   ____ c. will try to sting it.
   ____d. starts to buzz.

2. Bees work together very closely because
   ____a. they don't trust each other.
   ____b. the hive is crowded.
   ____ c. each has a special job to do for the hive.
   ____d. it helps them keep warm.

3. A bee must be a messenger so that she can
   ____a. tell important things to other bees.
   ____b. carry notes to the hive.
   ____ c. tell stories about bees she has met in other places.
   ____d. fly as far as she likes.

4. A man named Karl von Frisch
   ____a. lived a hundred years ago.
   ____b. thought bees were stupid.
   ____ c. wrote a book about clover.
   ____d. studied the language of the bees.

5. The "round dance" of the bees is done
   ____a. to amuse the other bees.
   ____b. to make the other bees join in a circle.
   ____ c. only when the bee finds clover.
   ____d. to tell the other bees that sweet food is near.

6. By dancing the "wagging dance," the bee
   ____a. shows that she wants to have a party.
   ____b. tells the others about food blossoms that are far away.
   ____ c. keeps the hive warm.
   ____d. tells the other bees where to put the honey.

7. When the "wagging dance" is very fast, it means that
   ____a. night is about to fall.
   ____b. the bee is in a hurry to finish the dance.
   ____ c. the other bees will have to fly far.
   ____d. the bee is a good dancer.

8. If bees did not dance,
   ____a. they would get more work done.
   ____b. they would have less fun.
   ____ c. they would have to find some other language.
   ____d. we would understand them better.

9. Another name for this story could be
   ____a. "How Bees Make Honey."
   ____b. "Language Is Used by Everyone."
   ____ c. "The Language of Honey Bees."
   ____d. "The Way Bees Have A Party."

10. This story is mainly about
   ____a. how bees sting.
   ____b. how bees "talk" together.
   ____ c. why bees fly.
   ____d. the color of bees.

Check your answers with the key on page 53.

Idea starter: How do people sometimes tell things to one another without using words?

The Dance Of The Bees

VOCABULARY CHECK

Use one of the key words from the box to complete each sentence.

| clover | discovery | distance | language | messenger | swarm |

1. The English _____ has a number of words that sound the same, but do not mean the same thing.

2. A _____ of bees flew by, making the children run away.

3. A _____ came from the king to tell the people that they would have a holiday.

4. From New York to Texas is a long _____ .

5. We found _____ growing in the meadow.

6. The _____ of oil in the West made many people go there in search of it.

Check your answers with the key on page 55.

The Old Man Who Dreamed His Fortune

Learn the Key Words

awoke	(ə wōk′)	to come out of sleep; awakened *He awoke after his dream.*
difficult	(dif′ ə kult)	not easy *The old pair had a difficult life because they were very poor.*
disappointment	(dis′ ə point mənt)	the feeling that comes over a person whose hopes fail *The fisherman felt great disappointment when he found no treasure in Chester.*
groan	(grōn)	a low, unhappy voice sound *The old man began to groan because digging is hard work.*
laughter	(laf′ tər)	the sound made by a laugh, usually after seeing or hearing something funny *The policeman broke into laughter when he learned why the old man was digging.*
wheelbarrow	(hwēl′ bar ō)	a kind of small cart with one wheel in the front and two handles in the rear for pushing and steering it *He took the wheelbarrow with him to Chester to carry back the gold.*

Preview:
1. Read the title.
2. Look at the picture.
3. Read the first paragraph of the story.
4. Then answer the following question.

You learned that
_____ a. the fisherman was rich.
_____ b. the fisherman was poor.
_____ c. the fisherman always had enough to eat.
_____ d. the fisherman had a comfortable home.

Turn to the Comprehension Check on page 14 for the right answer.

Now read the story.
Read to find out whose dream came true.

The Old Man Who Dreamed His Fortune

The old man hopes to fill his wheelbarrow with gold. Will he?

This is a story about a dream that came true. It is about a poor old fisherman who lived in a village called Surrey. In his dreams, he had a warm, comfortable home. It was not broken down, with the wind whistling through the cracks, like the house he lived in. Often, he and his wife had nothing more to eat than a bit of dry bread and sometimes some boiled fish. That happened when the fisherman was lucky enough to catch a fish. But in his dreams there was always a lot of good food to eat.

Over and over again the old man dreamed that some day he would be rich. He had that dream so often he believed it would come true.

"Some day our luck will change," he said to his wife. "My dreams have told me so."

His wife answered with a groan. It seemed to her that her whole life was filled with disappointment. "When do you expect this to happen?" she asked. "You are already sixty years old. Every day it grows more difficult for you to earn money. Do you expect a fortune to fall from the sky?"

"Perhaps, my dear," he answered. And then he lay down and took a little nap. He smiled in his sleep as he dreamed of sitting in a cozy chair and eating chicken and chocolate cake. His poor old wife sat there worrying as she sewed up the holes in his other pair of socks.

Suddenly, he awoke and sat up. "What a wonderful dream I just had!" he exclaimed. "I went to the village of Chester with a wheelbarrow and a shovel. By the big oak tree in the park, I dug a hole. And in the hole was a pile of gold. I brought it home and we were rich!''

His wife looked at him over the glasses she wore at the tip of her nose. She broke into laughter and said, ''My dear husband, your dreams are very silly.''

That night as they both lay in bed sleeping, the fisherman suddenly opened his eyes. His wife awoke when he called out, ''Wife, I have had the same dream again. I went to Chester and discovered gold. Tomorrow morning I must go to Chester.''

Nothing she said could make him change his mind. Early the next day he borrowed a wheelbarrow and a shovel. Then he walked to Chester, which was a few miles from Surrey. He knew exactly where to find the oak tree of his dreams because he had often visited Chester.

It was so early in the day that not many people were about. He took off his coat and began to dig. He dug and he dug, but he found no gold. Digging is difficult work. With a groan, he put down his shovel and lay down to rest. He felt full of disappointment.

Soon, he got up and got to work with the shovel again. As he started to dig, he heard an angry voice. He looked up and saw a policeman watching him. ''What's going on here?'' the policeman asked. ''Don't you know it's against the law to dig holes in the park?''

''Please, sir. All my life I have been poor, and this is my only chance to be rich,'' said the fisherman. And then he told about his dream.

The policeman broke into loud laughter. ''I had a dream like yours the other night,'' he said. ''I dreamed I was a fisherman, and that I lived in Surrey. In my dream I found a treasure under the floor of my house. Of course, when I awoke, I put the dream out of my mind, for I have good sense. I'm going to let you go. But listen to me — forget your dream.''

As the fisherman listened, he grew pale. ''Thank you for all you have told me,'' he said, picking up the shovel and putting it into the wheelbarrow.

He returned to Surrey as quickly as he could. As soon as he reached his house, he asked his wife to help him tear up the floor.

''Have you gone completely mad?'' she cried.

But she did as he asked. He began to dig, and soon his shovel struck something hard. In front of them lay a large wooden chest. The old man's hands shook as he opened it. The chest was filled with a fortune in gold!

With the gold, a new life began for the fisherman and his wife. They lived in a great big house they bought after they found the gold. From that time on, they had plenty to eat and everything else they needed.

The fisherman and his wife lived to be very, very old. Never again did his wife laugh at the fisherman for having foolish dreams.

The Old Man Who Dreamed His Fortune

COMPREHENSION CHECK

Choose the best answer.

1. The old fisherman lived in
    - ____a. Surrey, in a comfortable house.
    - ____b. Chester, near the park.
    - ____c. Surrey, in a house with cracks in it.
    - ____d. Chester, a small village.

2. The fisherman was certain he would be rich some day because
    - ____a. his dreams told him so.
    - ____b. there would be plenty of fish in the sea.
    - ____c. he had been poor long enough.
    - ____d. his wife wanted him to be rich.

3. His wife groaned because
    - ____a. she had a pain in her arm.
    - ____b. she did not like to sew.
    - ____c. she did not believe the fisherman's dreams.
    - ____d. she did not like boiled fish.

4. In his dream, the old man
    - ____a. took a wheelbarrow and a shovel to Chester.
    - ____b. took a wheelbarrow filled with gold to Chester.
    - ____c. rode in a wheelbarrow to Chester.
    - ____d. carried a large box to the next town.

5. The old man's wife laughed because
    - ____a. he looked so funny when he slept.
    - ____b. there were holes in his socks.
    - ____c. he told her a joke.
    - ____d. she thought his dreams were silly.

6. The fisherman felt full of disappointment in Chester because
    - ____a. his wheelbarrow broke down.
    - ____b. he found no gold under the oak tree.
    - ____c. there were so few people around.
    - ____d. the oak tree was in the wrong place.

7. The policeman was angry because
    - ____a. he found the old man digging holes in the park.
    - ____b. the old man talked back to him.
    - ____c. he wanted the gold for himself.
    - ____d. he had had a bad dream.

8. The old man turned pale and left quickly, because
    - ____a. he was afraid of what the policeman might do to him.
    - ____b. he began to feel ill.
    - ____c. he thought he was in trouble.
    - ____d. he saw that his fortune lay in the policeman's dream.

9. Another name for this story could be
    - ____a. "The Gold Under the Oak Tree."
    - ____b. "The Lucky Policeman."
    - ____c. "The Old Man Who Had No Hope."
    - ____d. "Dreams Sometimes Come True."

10. This story is mainly about
    - ____a. a shoemaker and his wife.
    - ____b. how to push a wheelbarrow.
    - ____c. dreams that came true.
    - ____d. the park in Surrey.

Check your answers with the key on page 53.

Idea starter: How would the story have ended if the fisherman didn't know about the policeman's dream?

The Old Man Who Dreamed His Fortune

VOCABULARY CHECK

Use a key word from the box to complete each of the sentences.

awoke	difficult	disappointment	groan	laughter	wheelbarrow

1. A _____ is helpful when moving heavy loads.

2. People sometimes feel sorry for themselves after a _____ .

3. An unhappy person might _____ .

4. Yesterday, when I _____ , I heard the birds singing.

5. Clowns did their funny tricks and the circus tent was filled with _____ .

6. Helen found that learning to skate was _____ .

Check your answers with the key on page 56.

Moby Maybe

Learn the Key Words

anger   (ang′ gər)   strong, unfriendly feelings
> *Joe showed his <u>anger</u> at striking out, by throwing his bat down.*

attention   (ə ten′ shən)   keeping one's mind on a thought
> *The class listened with <u>attention</u> as the teacher spoke.*

dock   (dok)   a place where ships land and tie up
> *Captain Barnes steered the boat towards the <u>dock</u>.*

fin   (fin)   a thin part on the outside of a fish's body that helps it move through the water
> *The killer whale has a large black <u>fin</u> on the middle of its back.*

leap   (lēp)   jump up
> *Carl had to <u>leap</u> high to catch the ball.*

wound   (wünd)
1. a place on the body where the skin has been opened
   > *Be sure to wash any dirt out of the <u>wound</u> on your leg.*

2. to hurt
   > *A sharp knife could easily <u>wound</u> the child.*

Preview:

1. Read the title.
2. Look at the picture.
3. Read the first paragraph of the story.
4. Then answer the following question.

You learned that
_____ a. Sam was riding in a truck.
_____ b. Sam was going to paint a picture.
_____ c. Sam wounded a whale.
_____ d. Sam killed a whale.

Turn to the Comprehension Check on page 19 for the right answer.

Now read the story.
Read to find out how smart a whale can be.

Moby Maybe

Sam is aiming his harpoon gun at a killer whale.

A place you will read about: Vancouver	(van kü′ vər)	a city near the Pacific Ocean
Things you will read about: harpoon gun	(här pün′ gun)	a gun that shoots spears
statue	(stach′ ü)	a piece of art that is made to look like a person or animal and that is usually made of stone, wood, clay, or metal

Sam leaned over the side of the boat, when he saw a huge black fin heading towards him. That fin told him it was a killer whale. Sam raised his harpoon gun, took aim, and fired. The knife at the end of the rope hit its mark. The whale leaped out of the water squeaking loudly. It was not dead, just wounded. Sam needed a dead whale as a model for the statue he was to make for the city of Vancouver.

The whale was swimming quietly on its line and would be easy to hit. Sam picked up his gun again, aimed, then stopped. An idea struck him! No killer whale had ever been caught and kept alive for doctors to study. This could be the first one. Sam had to work fast if he were to save the whale's life. He sent a radio call to Vancouver. He wanted doctors waiting at the dock with a salt water tank for the whale.

During the long trip back, Sam decided his whale ought to have a name. He remembered the famous whale story, *Moby Dick*, and thought that Moby Dick would be a good name. But what if it were a girl whale? Then Moby Doll might be better. Since Sam wasn't sure, he decided on Moby Maybe.

News about Sam and Moby

Maybe spread through the city quickly, and thousands of people were waiting at the dock to greet them. Doctors carefully took out the knife and gave the whale something to help its wound get better.

Sam spent many days sitting on a float in Moby Maybe's tank, keeping the whale company while it got better. A killer whale could easily break up a float with its tail if it wanted to, but Moby didn't. The whale seemed to know that Sam was its friend.

One thing did worry Sam. Moby wasn't eating. No matter what kind of meat or fish Sam offered, Moby refused everything. This went on for eight weeks.

Then, one day, the whale started flapping its tail as if to get Sam's attention. Sam threw Moby a fish, and the whale ate it. Then Sam threw two more, and Moby ate them, too. Crowds around Moby's tank cheered. Stories about Moby's first meal appeared on the front page of every Vancouver newspaper. Moby had become the city's pet, and news that the whale had eaten, made the whole city happy.

Soon, Moby was eating one hundred pounds of fish every day. The whale, who had been quiet and shy before, now leaped and played in the water.

One day, Sam announced lunch by slapping the water with the fish that Moby liked best — cod. Moby swam up to Sam, took the fish from him, and ate it. Then Sam held the next fish high in the air to get the whale to leap for it. Moby took one look at where Sam was holding the fish and quickly dived under the water.

The whale came up on the other side of the tank flapping its tail in anger. When Sam lowered the fish closer to the water, Moby came back and took it.

Next, Sam splashed the water with a rockfish. Moby took one look at the sharp fins on the fish's body and swam away. The whale showed its anger again by flapping its tail. But when Sam had cut off the sharp fins, Moby returned and ate the fish. Sam was discovering just how smart Moby was. The whale had a mind of its own! Moby was training Sam, instead of Sam training Moby.

The doctors were eager to test Moby's hearing, for they knew that whales have a very sharp sense of hearing. They played recordings of calls of other killer whales for Moby. When the whale heard them, it answered them with excited squeaks. But when doctors played a recording of Moby's own voice, the whale paid no attention to it at all.

After a few months, Moby's shiny black skin started turning gray. The doctors began to worry. They found that the trouble was with the water in the tank. It wasn't as salty as the ocean water. Plans were made to move Moby's tank to another dock where the water was better.

But before the tank could be moved, Moby took one last dive. The mighty killer whale never came up again. Divers went into the tank and discovered the whale dead at the bottom. They also discovered that Moby Maybe was really Moby Doll!

Sam finally made his statue for the city of Vancouver. But to him, it was not just a statue of a killer whale. It was a way to honor Moby Doll. For she had taught the world just how clever killer whales really are.

Moby Maybe

COMPREHENSION CHECK

| **Preview answer:** |
| c. Sam wounded a whale. |

Choose the best answer.

1. When Sam shot the whale,
   ____a. it dived under the water quickly.
   ____b. it leaped out of the water squeaking.
   ____c. it attacked his boat with its tail.
   ____d. it broke the line and swam away.

2. Sam was out hunting a whale
   ____a. to keep as a family pet.
   ____b. to study how whales behave.
   ____c. to use as a model for a statue.
   ____d. to teach it to do tricks.

3. Sam decided not to kill the whale because
   ____a. he wanted to let doctors study it.
   ____b. his gun wasn't working too well.
   ____c. the people of Vancouver didn't want him to.
   ____d. he was afraid other whales would attack him.

4. Sam named the whale Moby Maybe because
   ____a. Moby was Sam's last name.
   ____b. it was the name of a famous whale story.
   ____c. the doctors thought it was a good name.
   ____d. he wasn't sure if it was a boy or girl whale.

5. Vancouver newspapers had stories of Moby on the front page because
   ____a. there was no other news to print.
   ____b. people were very interested in the whale.
   ____c. Sam asked them to put it there.
   ____d. that was where they always put animal stories.

6. After the whale started eating,
   ____a. it leaped and played in the water.
   ____b. it became quiet and shy.
   ____c. it attacked Sam and the doctors.
   ____d. it flapped its tail in anger.

7. Moby got angry when Sam
   ____a. slapped the water with a fish.
   ____b. held the fish high in the air.
   ____c. sat on a float in the tank.
   ____d. cut off the sharp fins on the fish.

8. When doctors played recordings of other whales' voices,
   ____a. Moby paid no attention to them.
   ____b. Moby swam away in anger.
   ____c. Moby leaped out of the water.
   ____d. Moby answered with excited squeaks.

9. Another name for this story could be
   ____a. "Sam, The Whale Hunter."
   ____b. "How to Feed Killer Whales."
   ____c. "The Clever Killer Whale."
   ____d. "Animal Doctors at Work."

10. This story is mainly about
    ____a. the different kinds of fish killer whales eat.
    ____b. catching whales off the coast of Vancouver.
    ____c. things doctors learned by studying a killer whale.
    ____d. a killer whale's sharp sense of hearing.

Check your answers with the key on page 53.

Idea starter: How do animals sometimes train people?

Moby Maybe

VOCABULARY CHECK

Choose the best answer to each riddle.

1. I'm a feeling that you sometimes get,
    When things don't go your way;
    I make you scream, or cry, or fight,
    Or say some things you shouldn't say.

    I am
    _____ a. fear.   _____ c. anger.
    _____ b. surprise.   _____ d. happiness.

2. I'm on the body of a fish,
    I stick up from its skin;
    I help it move below the sea,
    My shape is flat and thin.

    I am a
    _____ a. mouth.   _____ c. bone.
    _____ b. fin.   _____ d. tail.

3. You do this when you have to reach,
    A tall branch on a tree;
    You bend your legs, then up you go,
    And come down carefully.

    You would be
    _____ a. falling.   _____ c. sitting.
    _____ b. walking.   _____ d. leaping.

4. It happens to some people,
    With a stick, or knife, or gun;
    They usually get better,
    Once a doctor's work is done.

    These people would be
    _____ a. wounded.   _____ c. caught.
    _____ b. killed.   _____ d. hungry.

5. I stick out from the shore line,
    On a river, lake, or sea;
    Captains steer their boats up close,
    Then tie them on to me.

    I am a
    _____ a. sail.   _____ c. dock.
    _____ b. pool.   _____ d. diving board.

6. It's important that it's with you,
    When you're learning something new;
    It keeps your mind on each new thought,
    To help you think and do.

    It is
    _____ a. attention.   _____ c. excitement.
    _____ b. sleep.   _____ d. courage.

Check your answers with the key on page 56.

An Unexpected Visitor

Learn the Key Words

avoid   (ə void′)   to stay away from
When Billy was angry with his friends, he tried to <u>avoid</u> them.

grateful   (grāt′ fəl)   full of thanks
Betty was <u>grateful</u> for the new toys her father gave her.

interrupt   (in tə rupt′)   break in on someone's talking, work, or rest
It is not polite to <u>interrupt</u> someone who is talking.

opinion   (ə pin′ yən)   a strong belief
It was the teacher's <u>opinion</u> that the children could do the work that she gave them.

racket   (rak′ it)   a loud noise
There was a terrible <u>racket</u> when the pots and pans fell on the floor.

scamper   (skam′ pər)   to run or move quickly
The kittens would <u>scamper</u> to their mother when someone came near them.

Preview:

1. Read the title.
2. Look at the picture.
3. Read the first paragraph of the story.
4. Then answer the following question.

You learned that this story
_____ a. takes place in a field.
_____ b. takes place in a bedroom.
_____ c. takes place in a classroom.
_____ d. takes place in a city.

Turn to the Comprehension Check on page 24 for the right answer.

Now read the story.
Read to find out why the visitor returned to its home.

An Unexpected Visitor

A few minutes ago, these boys and girls weren't paying attention. Now everyone is interested in what is happening.

The class in Room 17 was having trouble paying attention to Mrs. Marshall's lesson. They were not comfortable in the hot room. They turned in their seats and gazed out the window at the sunny day. They could see bright flowers in the fields outside. They could hear the birds making a racket with their loud singing.

Andrea was one of those who had stopped listening to Mrs. Marshall. She was watching a bee on the edge of a flower near the window. Suddenly, her attention turned to something moving quickly along the floor. Andrea watched it scamper across the front of the room.

"It's a mouse!" she called out. "There's a mouse near Mrs. Marshall's desk!"

What excitement followed! What a racket there was as boys and girls shouted and laughed.

David and Karen jumped out of their seats and chased the mouse. The other children called out,

"He's over there!"

"No, he's going the other way!"

"Hurry, or you'll never catch him!"

Mrs. Marshall, who had jumped out of the way to avoid the running children, tried to quiet the class. "Children, please calm down! I'd be

grateful if you'd be quiet! Be seated, please!" But there was so much noise that no one could hear her.

Almost all the children were now trying to catch the mouse. No sooner did they think they had him in a corner, then he would scamper off in another direction. He led them in a wild chase all over the room and then disappeared behind a heavy bookcase. They waited for him, but he did not come out of his hiding place.

"That's enough!" called Mrs. Marshall. "Back to your seats, everyone. We have let that mouse interrupt our work long enough."

But the children were too excited to return to work. Everyone wanted to talk about the mouse. Mrs. Marshall gave in, and soon everyone was giving his and her opinion on how to catch the mouse.

"I think we should get some cheese and put it near the shelf," said Janie.

"I know how to build a trap," offered John. "I could build one and bring it to school tomorrow. We could put the cheese in the trap."

The children thought that was a good idea until Andrea pointed out that a trap could hurt the mouse or even kill it. She was sorry that she had ever seen the mouse in the first place.

"Why don't we just leave the mouse alone?" she asked. "He'll find his way home if we just don't bother him."

"In my opinion, the sooner that mouse is out of here, the better it will be for all of us," replied Mrs. Marshall.

"How do you think the mouse got in here in the first place?" Karen wanted to know.

The children thought about it. Then Jody said, "I think I know. Our mouse must be a field mouse. He probably lives in the field right outside the school. He must have wandered in here by mistake, and now he's lost and can't find his way home."

"Yes," agreed Mrs. Marshall, "I think you are right. The problem now is to get him out of here quickly. We want to avoid any more trouble."

The children thought for a while. Finally, they all agreed upon a plan. First, Karen took cheese out of her lunch box and placed it on the floor near the shelf where the mouse was hiding. Then David held the door wide open. The other children pushed their desks and chairs to the sides of the room leaving a clear path from the shelf to the open door. They lined up near the mouse's hiding place and waited for him to appear. They waited and waited, but nothing happened.

"Maybe he ate already, and he's not hungry," said Karen.

"Maybe he . . .," began Tony, when David interrupted him and said, "Quiet, here he comes!"

And sure enough, a little nose and whiskers were peeking around the corner of the bookcase. Two little eyes looked around carefully. The children stood as still and quiet as they could. At last the mouse came out and began to nibble at the cheese. Suddenly, the boys and girls began to shout and yell. The mouse looked up, startled, and dashed across the floor. The children chased him towards the front of the room and, just as they had hoped, he ran out the door. They chased him through the open front door of the school and watched him scamper into the field, back to his home.

"Well, that's that," said Mrs. Marshall, grateful that the excitement was over. "Now we can get back to work."

The children sat down, but it was a long time before they thought of anything but the visit from the little field mouse.

An Unexpected Visitor

COMPREHENSION CHECK

Choose the best answer.

1. This story most likely takes place before which vacation?
   ____a.   Summer.
   ____b.   Spring.
   ____c.   Thanksgiving.
   ____d.   Winter.

2. The children had trouble listening to the lesson because
   ____a.   they didn't like the teacher.
   ____b.   they didn't have to.
   ____c.   they were not comfortable.
   ____d.   it was not an interesting lesson.

3. Andrea didn't want to use a mouse trap because
   ____a.   she didn't think it would work.
   ____b.   she wanted the mouse to stay in the room.
   ____c.   she didn't want the mouse to be harmed.
   ____d.   it would take too much time.

4. The plan to get rid of the mouse was agreed to by
   ____a.   Mrs. Marshall.
   ____b.   all the children.
   ____c.   Andrea.
   ____d.   David and Karen.

5. The children were very quiet while they waited for the mouse to come out of hiding because
   ____a.   they didn't want to bother him.
   ____b.   they didn't want him to be afraid to come out.
   ____c.   Mrs. Marshall told them to be quiet.
   ____d.   they were tired of shouting.

6. The mouse came out of his hiding place
   ____a.   to eat the cheese.
   ____b.   to frighten the teacher.
   ____c.   to get out of the classroom.
   ____d.   to run around the room.

7. The mouse probably came into the room
   ____a.   to get out of the sun.
   ____b.   to get some cheese.
   ____c.   to visit the children.
   ____d.   by mistake.

8. Mrs. Marshall was glad the mouse was gone because
   ____a.   the children didn't like the mouse.
   ____b.   she wanted to get back to work.
   ____c.   it was too hot to chase a mouse.
   ____d.   mice are not allowed in school.

9. Another name for this story could be
   ____a.   "How to Catch Mice."
   ____b.   "A Warm Day in School."
   ____c.   "A Mouse Comes to Visit."
   ____d.   "Building a Mouse Trap."

10. This story is mainly about
   ____a.   a teacher trying to teach a lesson.
   ____b.   a noisy class.
   ____c.   how a mouse got into a classroom.
   ____d.   what happened when a mouse visited a classroom.

Check your answers with the key on page 53.

Idea starter: What animals would be good to have in a classroom?

An Unexpected Visitor

VOCABULARY CHECK

Choose a key word from the box to complete each of the following sentences.

avoid	grateful	interrupt	opinion	racket	scamper

1. We should be _____ for the good things we have.

2. That loud noise will _____ Dad's nap.

3. Sally tries to _____ playing ball because she doesn't play very well.

4. Mrs. Smith wasn't happy with the _____ the noisy children were making.

5. It's fun to watch the little children _____ away from the waves on the beach.

6. "It's my _____ ," said Jane, "that dogs make the best pets."

Check your answers with the key on page 57.

Why The Stars Stopped Singing

Learn the Key Words

bracelet (brās' lit)   an ornament in the form of a circle, worn on the arm
Elsie cried when she saw that her <u>bracelet</u> was missing from her arm.

cobbler (cob' lər)   someone who repairs or makes shoes
The <u>cobbler</u> made many pairs of shoes with the pretty buttons.

creature (krē' chər)   a living being
Elsie was a shy <u>creature</u> and did not make friends easily.

graze (grāz)   1. to feed on grass and plants growing out of the ground
Sheep and cows <u>graze</u> in the meadow grass.

2. to touch or rub lightly
See his long horn <u>graze</u> the sky.

stole (stōl)   1. to have taken something that belongs to someone else
A thief <u>stole</u> our TV set.

2. a scarf worn around the shoulders
Elsie wore a <u>stole</u> because she was cold.

unicorn (yü' nə kôrn)   a make-believe animal that looks like a horse and has a long, straight horn growing out of its head
Although there is so no such animal as a <u>unicorn</u>, I read a story about one.

Preview:

1. Read the title.
2. Look at the picture.
3. Read the first two paragraphs of the story.
4. Then answer the following question.

You learned that this story is about
_____ a. the silent stars.
_____ b. a village in England.
_____ c. an unusual animal.
_____ d. a horn that people could blow.

Turn to the Comprehension Check on page 29 for the right answer.

Now read the story.
Read to find out why stars no longer sing.

Why The Stars Stopped Singing

When this unicorn's horn reached the stars, beautiful singing could be heard.

Did you know that there was a time, years ago, when the stars in the sky used to sing?

Many years ago, the stars sang because of a unicorn. The unicorn lived in a large forest near a small village in England. Even in those days, unicorns were very unusual creatures. And this one was unusual even for a unicorn. His horn was so long it reached up into the sky. When his horn touched the stars, they would start to sing.

During the day, the unicorn would graze. He ate grass, berries, and the wild flowers that grew in the forest. At night, he sat on the ground with his head raised to the sky as he smelled the sweet, fresh air.

His horn would graze the stars, and then the stars sang. Sad people became happy when they heard the stars singing. Babies stopped crying and fell asleep when they heard the stars singing. People who were ill began to feel better when they heard the stars singing.

"Life would not be the same without the unicorn," everyone said.

One afternoon, as the unicorn grazed in the forest, he noticed a girl sitting on a stone and crying. The unicorn was a friendly creature with a kind heart. He couldn't stand seeing anyone cry. So he asked, "What is your name, little girl, and why are you unhappy?"

The little girl was so astonished to hear the unicorn talk that she stopped crying. She wiped her eyes with the yellow stole she wore around her neck. "I'm Elsie," she said shyly. "I've lost my bracelet and I can't find it. My father will be angry with me. He carved it just for me out of wood," she explained.

"I know what we can do," the unicorn said. "Your father can make you another bracelet from a piece of my horn. Cut off a little bit. It won't hurt me. But, please, promise me that you will not tell anyone where you got the horn."

"Thank you, dear unicorn. I promise not to tell anyone. And

I have a gift for you. Here is my yellow stole.'' And off she ran, leaving the unicorn to wonder what to do with the scarf hanging from his horn.

Elsie ran home to show the unicorn's gift to her father. She was so excited that she forgot her promise to the unicorn. She told her father how she happened to have a piece of unicorn horn. Her father made her a new bracelet that was even more beautiful than the old one. Elsie's father was a cobbler, and while he worked on Elsie's bracelet, he had been thinking of the wonderful shoe buttons he could make from the unicorn's horn.

Finally, the cobbler went to the unicorn and said, ''Please, dear unicorn, I am a poor cobbler. If I had a piece of your horn, I could make wonderful buttons for my shoes. Many people would want to buy them. I would be able to have more money to buy food and clothing for my wife and children.''

The unicorn sighed. He thought, ''How hard it is for people to keep a secret.'' But he felt sorry for the cobbler and let him cut a few inches off his horn.

The cobbler sold many pairs of shoes made with buttons from the unicorn's horn. Soon, everyone in the village knew how the cobbler was able to make such wonderful buttons. Many people went to the unicorn, asking him for bits of his horn. They wanted the horn to make things like rings and bracelets and combs and boxes.

At first, the unicorn let the people have all they wanted. But then he begged them to leave him alone. Then the mayor of the village heard about the people going to the unicorn. He ordered them to stay away from the unicorn. But people went to the unicorn anyway. While he slept, they stole pieces of his horn. The more they stole, the shorter the unicorn's horn became. It became too short to reach the sky.

The unicorn's horn was no longer able to graze the stars, and they stopped singing. The people of the village were very unhappy. They knew that they had lost their lovely night music because they were so greedy. But it was too late to do anything about it.

Why The Stars Stopped Singing

COMPREHENSION CHECK

Choose the best answer.

1. The stars sang
   ____a. when the moon came out.
   ____b. when the unicorn's horn grazed them.
   ____c. because they were twinkling.
   ____d. only on holidays.

2. The unicorn
   ____a. looked just like other unicorns.
   ____b. lived in the zoo.
   ____c. was kind and friendly.
   ____d. was unpleasant to everyone.

3. Elsie was crying because she
   ____a. had lost her bracelet.
   ____b. was feeling ill.
   ____c. had lost her way in the forest.
   ____d. had a fight with her father.

4. Elsie promised the unicorn
   ____a. to come back again.
   ____b. to give him her money.
   ____c. that she would keep a secret.
   ____d. that she would not hurt him.

5. Elsie's father made for her
   ____a. new shoes.
   ____b. a bracelet.
   ____c. a doll house.
   ____d. a box.

6. The cobbler wanted some of the unicorn's horn to make
   ____a. a pipe.
   ____b. a ring.
   ____c. a comb.
   ____d. buttons.

7. When the mayor gave an order,
   ____a. everyone kept away from the unicorn.
   ____b. the unicorn was locked in jail.
   ____c. the people stopped buying shoes.
   ____d. some people stole from the unicorn anyway.

8. When the unicorn's horn became short,
   ____a. he looked like a cow.
   ____b. everyone went home.
   ____c. life was no longer the same.
   ____d. the people were happy.

9. Another name for this story could be
   ____a. "What to Feed a Unicorn."
   ____b. "How Elsie Got a Bracelet."
   ____c. "How the Unicorn Got a Stole."
   ____d. "The Unicorn Who Gave Too Much."

10. The main idea of this story is that
   ____a. greed makes people destroy nature.
   ____b. unicorns make good pets.
   ____c. stars don't really sing.
   ____d. things were better in the old days.

Check your answers with the key on page 53.

Idea starter: If stars sang, what would their music be like?

Why The Stars Stopped Singing

VOCABULARY CHECK

Complete each sentence by writing in the correct key word from the box.

bracelet	cobbler	creature	graze	stole	unicorn

1. My mother used green wool to knit a _____ .

2. The _____ was a make-believe creature.

3. In the summer, farmers take their animals outdoors to _____ .

4. A robber _____ money from the bank.

5. My _____ fell off my arm and was lost.

6. Did you see the car _____ against the bus?

7. Many a strange _____ swims in the sea.

8. The _____ put new heels on my shoes.

Check your answers with the key on page 57.

Courage On The Court

Learn the Key Words

court	(kôrt, kōrt)	1. a place marked off for playing a game *Hoops were set up at both ends of the <u>court</u> for the basketball game.* 2. a place where questions of law are decided
develop	(di vel′ əp)	become better or larger *An average dancer can <u>develop</u> into a good dancer through practice.*
perfect	(per′ fikt)	without faults; correct *Dr. Hoffman said Lisa's weight was <u>perfect</u> for her age.*
position	(pə zish′ ən)	1. a way of holding the body *The catcher bent down in his <u>position</u> behind home plate.* 2. the place where someone or something is 3. a job
quarter	(kwôr′ tər)	1. one of four parts that is the same size or time as the other three parts *Jeff was hurt during the second <u>quarter</u> of the football game.* 2. a silver U.S. coin worth 25¢
realize	(rē′ ə līz)	understand clearly *It was difficult for little Sandy to <u>realize</u> her dog had died.*

Preview:

1. Read the title.
2. Look at the picture.
3. Read the first paragraph of the story.
4. Then answer the following question.

You learned from your preview that
_____ a. a basketball game was about to be played.
_____ b. a basketball game had been played.
_____ c. a basketball game was being played.
_____ d. a large crowd was at the basketball court.

Turn to the Comprehension Check on page 34 for the right answer.

Now read the story
Read to find out what made Brad such a special player.

Courage On The Court

A basketball coach will soon be told a secret that he'll always remember.

Places you will read about:	Bryant High School
	Long Island City High School
People you will read about:	Lou Hacker
	Bradshaw Lincoln
	Rick Barnes
Something you will read about:	hook shot

The game had ended hours ago. Bryant High School was dark except for one light that still burned on the basketball court. Coach Lou Hacker sat on a bench, staring at the empty court and thinking about the game.

Lou knew that as long as he coached basketball, he would always remember the star of today's game, Bradshaw Lincoln.

Lou first saw Brad when the boy came to try out for the basketball team. That was two years ago. Brad was not a good shooter, but he ran well and passed well. Because he loved the game and never missed a practice, Brad had developed into a good team player.

Today's game had been a big one for Bryant High School. It was against Long Island City High School. During the season, both teams had won sixteen games and lost only one. But Bryant had never been able to beat Long Island City. Today's game would decide the best of all the New York City high school teams. Lou planned to use Brad in the game, but he knew he had to depend on his star shooters if he hoped to win.

During the first three quarters, each team kept the other from making too many baskets. First Bryant led, then Long Island City went ahead. The two teams were never more than three or four points apart.

With only one minute left to play in the last quarter, each team had forty-five points. Both teams realized that there was time for only one more play. The team that made the next basket would be the winner.

A Long Island City player had the ball. When he tried to pass it to another player, Brad jumped up and grabbed it. He passed it to Rick Barnes, Bryant's star shooter. As Rick turned with the ball, he found himself too closely guarded to try a shot. Only ten seconds remained in the game. Rick looked around to see to whom he could pass. He hoped to pass to one of the good shooters in position under the basket. But they were all too closely guarded. The only player in the clear was Brad. Rick passed the ball off to Brad who was still twenty feet away from the basket.

Eight seconds remained. Brad caught the pass and bounced the ball towards the center of the court. His guard now stood between him and the basket.

Brad had no way to get into position to aim his shot. Six seconds remained. Brad turned and faced sideways. Lou realized that Brad was going to try for a hook shot. But the boy's head was turned in a strange position. It was not the usual position for a hook shot. Lou was puzzled. But up went Brad's left arm, hooking the ball high over his head. Up, up it sailed through the air and dropped right into the basket. A perfect shot! Good for two points! At that moment, the bell sounded. The game was over. Bryant had won 47 to 45.

The players crowded around a smiling Brad. The rest of the team jumped off the bench and joined in. Bryant High School fans were screaming and cheering. Lou made his way through the crowd onto the court. He shook Brad's hand and patted him on the back. "You had me scared there for a few seconds," Lou shouted over the noise of the crowd. "What was the big idea of turning your head the way you did before your shot?"

Brad's smile turned into a serious look. He turned to his coach and said, "Well, Coach, that was the only way I could see to make the shot. I guess it's about time I told you. I'm blind in one eye!"

Lou was astonished. The boy had been playing for two years and nobody ever knew. But before Lou could say another word, the team had lifted Brad up in the air and headed for the dressing room with their hero.

Now, as Lou sat on the empty court, he remembered the talk he had with Brad after the other boys had all gone home. Brad told him that he had been blind in one eye for many years. He had never told anyone at school, for he didn't want to be treated differently from the other boys. He had practiced hard and developed most of his movements so they looked as perfect as any boy's with two good eyes. Brad begged Lou not to tell anyone. Lou couldn't refuse. He gave the boy his promise.

Because of that promise, no one at Bryant High School ever knew just what kind of hero Bradshaw Lincoln really was. But to Coach Lou Hacker, Brad's courage and spirit made him a very special kind of hero.

Courage On The Court

COMPREHENSION CHECK

Choose the best answer.

1. The game took place on a basketball court
   ____a. at Long Island City High School.
   ____b. at Lincoln High School.
   ____c. at Bryant High School.
   ____d. in a New York City park.

2. Lou Hacker was
   ____a. the coach for Bryant High School.
   ____b. the coach for Long Island City High School.
   ____c. the star shooter of Bryant High School.
   ____d. the center for Long Island City High School.

3. Brad developed into a good team player because
   ____a. Lou depended on him.
   ____b. he loved the game.
   ____c. the team taught him.
   ____d. he was a star shooter.

4. With only a minute to play in the last quarter, Rick passed the ball to Brad because
   ____a. Brad was the best shooter on the team.
   ____b. Brad called for the ball.
   ____c. Lou told him to pass to Brad.
   ____d. Brad was the only player in the clear.

5. When Brad took a hook shot, Lou was puzzled because
   ____a. Brad never practiced hook shots.
   ____b. the bell had already sounded.
   ____c. Brad's head was in a strange position.
   ____d. Brad was too far from the basket.

6. Brad never told anyone he was blind in one eye because
   ____a. his mother told him not to.
   ____b. he wanted to be treated like other boys.
   ____c. his coach wanted to keep it a secret.
   ____d. his doctor wasn't sure of it himself.

7. The Bryant team lifted Brad high in the air because
   ____a. they wanted to get him away from Lou.
   ____b. they wanted him to reach the basket.
   ____c. they wanted to keep the fans away from him.
   ____d. they were proud of him.

8. Brad probably developed most of his movements by
   ____a. watching how boys with perfect eyesight moved.
   ____b. watching other people who were partly blind.
   ____c. going to a special school for blind children.
   ____d. listening to his coach talking to the team.

9. Another name for this story could be
   ____a. "A Blind Basketball Coach."
   ____b. "A Clever Player."
   ____c. "A Special Kind of Hero."
   ____d. "A Star Shooter."

10. This story is mainly about
   ____a. a basketball star who made many points for his team.
   ____b. a basketball coach who hated losing games.
   ____c. a basketball team that couldn't win games.
   ____d. a basketball player with courage and team spirit.

Check your answers with the key on page 53.

Idea starter: Why did the coach feel he had to keep Brad's secret?

Courage On The Court

VOCABULARY CHECK

Choose the answer that means the same as the underlined key word.

1. Mark's teacher smiled when she said his test paper was <u>perfect</u>.
   - _____ a. Wrong
   - _____ b. Funny
   - _____ c. Correct
   - _____ d. Hard

2. Tom broke his candy bar into <u>quarters</u>.
   - _____ a. Two parts the same size
   - _____ b. Four parts the same size
   - _____ c. One big piece and one small piece
   - _____ d. Hundreds of tiny pieces

3. Mr. Gaines tried to make his workers <u>realize</u> how important safety was on the job.
   - _____ a. Understand
   - _____ b. Complain
   - _____ c. Deserve
   - _____ d. Wonder

4. One hour of exercise every day can help your body <u>develop</u>.
   - _____ a. Get better
   - _____ b. Get old
   - _____ c. Get weak
   - _____ d. Get tired

5. The team had to be on the <u>court</u> for practice at 3:00 P.M.
   - _____ a. A place for swimming
   - _____ b. A place where animals live
   - _____ c. A place where people sleep
   - _____ d. A place where games are played

6. Wait until I get into <u>position</u> before you take my picture.
   - _____ a. A new dress
   - _____ b. A comfortable chair
   - _____ c. A way of holding the body
   - _____ d. A funny face

Check your answers with the key on page 58.

This page may be reproduced for classroom use.

Rescue At Sea!

Learn the Key Words

crew (krü)   men needed to do the work on a ship
The crew raised the sails on the boat.

dangerous (dān′ jər əs)   not safe; likely to cause harm
It is dangerous to jump from that tree.

hurricane (hėr′ ə kān)   a storm with strong winds and heavy rain
The hurricane knocked down many trees.

thankful (thangk′ fəl)   feeling pleased or grateful for something
We should be thankful for our friends.

voyage (voi′ ij)   a trip on the water
It is a long voyage from here to that island.

Wednesday (wenz′ dē, wenz′ dā)   the fourth day of the week
She will visit her friend on Wednesday.

Preview:

1. Read the title.
2. Look at the picture.
3. Read the first paragraph of the story.
4. Then answer the following question.

You learned from your preview that
_____ a. the "Butterfly" left Bermuda for New York.
_____ b. the "Butterfly" left New York for Bermuda.
_____ c. the "Butterfly" did not have a motor.
_____ d. strong winds were blowing.

Turn to the Comprehension Check on page 39 for the right answer.

Now read the story.
Read to find out why the men left the "Butterfly."

Rescue At Sea!

The "Butterfly" is in serious trouble now that it is caught in a hurricane.

Captain John had five young men as his crew. They set sail late in the afternoon of Saturday, June 26, 1975, from the island of Bermuda. All six had vacationed there since Wednesday, resting and enjoying themselves. At the start of their voyage, the ocean was as smooth as glass. Each of the six men was eager to begin the pleasant journey home to New York. Because there was no sign of a breeze, Captain John ran the motor of his sailboat, "Butterfly," both day and night.

When the wind picked up on Sunday, several of the crew raised the sails of the "Butterfly." They enjoyed most of the day, thankful for the gentle breeze. They watched the flying fish and the birds that followed them. By afternoon, the winds grew stronger, and as they did, the waves grew larger in size. In the evening, clouds covered the sky and rain began. By Sunday night, the storm had become a hurricane, and the six men were in serious danger.

A hurricane is the most dangerous of all large storms. In these storms there are heavy rains and strong winds that travel at speeds of seventy-five miles or more an hour. These dangerous winds cause damage over a great distance to everything in their path. The "Butterfly," a small boat about thirty feet long, could easily be wrecked by a hurricane.

Because of the high winds and the rough seas, Captain John and four of the crew became seasick and were not able to do much work. This left only one young man, Howard, in charge of steering the "Butterfly." Howard had never sailed a boat before, but he took charge for six hours while his friends rested. The little boat was tossed and thrown about by waves. The rain continued to hammer down.

Howard began to lose hope of ever being saved. As he grew more tired, he began to think that he and his friends would drown. Even as he thought this, things began to go wrong. Late Sunday night, one of the sails began to split. Shortly after this, the radio stopped working, making it impossible for Howard to reach another ship. Not too much later, Howard noticed that the small boat was beginning to fill with water.

The sea began to break over the "Butterfly." Howard thought it would be just a matter of time before they would all be lost at sea. He knew that the "Butterfly" had been blown off its course. He had little hope of someone rescuing them.

At one o'clock Monday morning, Captain John was finally able to help Howard. He took over the wheel of the "Butterfly," asking Howard to tie him into a chair so that he would not be thrown into the water. When Howard shouted his fears, Captain John refused to listen. Instead, the captain tried to calm Howard, telling him he should never give up hope. Captain John continued to talk to Howard over the roar of the ocean, telling him that men had worked their way through more terrible problems than this. He said they would be saved only if they worked hard and did not give up hope.

It was hours later when Captain John first spotted the light of a ship in the distance. As he headed his boat toward the light, Howard tried to radio again. To his surprise, he reached the other ship.

The men on the "Butterfly" were amazed at the size of the other ship as it came near. It was a huge ship from Russia, many times larger than the "Butterfly," and was far safer in a hurricane.

Over the radio, the men made plans for their rescue. By using large ropes, the crew from the Russian ship would lift them to safety. Howard, swinging in the strong wind, was the first man lifted over the wild water. He landed safely on the larger ship, and the other men followed. Captain John was the last to leave the "Butterfly."

When the six men were safe on the Russian ship, they danced and shouted with joy. The Russian men were kind. They gave them food and warm clothing, and allowed them to sleep in the most comfortable rooms. They all continued the voyage to New York. The Russian ship arrived there on Wednesday, the storm far behind. The thankful crew of the "Butterfly" shook hands with their Russian friends, grateful to them for their kindness. Then the men from the "Butterfly" shook hands with Captain John and Howard, thanking them. The men realized that the courage and hope of Captain John and Howard had helped save their lives.

Rescue At Sea!

COMPREHENSION CHECK

Choose the best answer.

1. Captain John's boat, the "Butterfly,"
   ____a. ran only by motor.
   ____b. had both motor and sails.
   ____c. was huge in size.
   ____d. had no motor.

2. In a hurricane
   ____a. there is no wind.
   ____b. there is no rain.
   ____c. there are strong winds and rain.
   ____d. there is little danger.

3. Howard and his friends
   ____a. were on vacation.
   ____b. lived in Bermuda.
   ____c. worked in Bermuda.
   ____d. did not like ships.

4. The "Butterfly" was blown
   ____a. back to Bermuda.
   ____b. off course.
   ____c. near an English ship.
   ____d. to New York.

5. The young man named Howard
   ____a. very often steered ships.
   ____b. did not like sailing.
   ____c. was very seasick.
   ____d. had never steered a ship before.

6. The men were rescued
   ____a. by a Russian ship.
   ____b. by a small boat.
   ____c. by a sea plane.
   ____d. when the storm was over.

7. The men on the rescue ship
   ____a. were not friendly or kind.
   ____b. were in great danger from the storm.
   ____c. were lost at sea.
   ____d. gave Captain John and his crew the most comfortable rooms.

8. When Captain John saw the light of the huge ship,
   ____a. he was more frightened than before.
   ____b. he thought that they would drown.
   ____c. he thought that they might be rescued.
   ____d. he was angry with Howard for not seeing it.

9. Another name for this story could be
   ____a. "Travel in Bermuda."
   ____b. "Courage at Sea."
   ____c. "Hurricanes."
   ____d. "How to Sail a Ship."

10. This story is mainly about
    ____a. the danger of travel by ship.
    ____b. Bermuda as a vacation island.
    ____c. Russian rescue ships.
    ____d. not giving up hope when faced with difficulty.

Check your answers with the key on page 53.

Idea starter: What are some of the things that Captain John might have said to Howard?

Rescue At Sea!

VOCABULARY CHECK

I.   *Use the key words in the box to complete the puzzle.*

crew	dangerous	hurricane	thankful	voyage	Wednesday

Across

1.   A day of the week
4.   Men who work on a ship
5.   A strong wind and rain storm

Down

2.   Not safe, likely to cause harm
3.   A trip on the water

II.   *Fill in the blank in each sentence with the correct key word from the box above.*

1.   On the day of the picnic, we were _____ for the sun.

2.   The weather man warned us of the _____ .

3.   The _____ worked all day painting the ship.

4.   Because of all the traffic, it is _____ to cross the street.

5.   The _____ from Bermuda to New York began on a Saturday.

6.   The Russian ship arrived in New York on a _____ .

Check your answers with the key on page 58.

Life In An Ant Colony

Learn the Key Words

burrow	(bėr′ ō)	to dig or make a hole *I saw the animal burrow under the ground.*
colony	(kol′ ə nē)	a place where a group of animals or people live near each other and work to help each other *Many ants live in a colony.*
familiar	(fə mil′ yər)	well-known *I saw a familiar face.*
garbage	(gär′ bij)	something that we throw away *Please take out the garbage.*
human	(hyü′ mən)	a person, or something having to do with a person *Man is a human being.*
reservation	(rez ər vā′ shən)	land set aside for a special reason *Some Indians still live on a reservation.*

Preview:

1. Read the title.
2. Look at the picture.
3. Read the first paragraph of the story.
4. Read the underlined sentences in the story.
5. Then answer the following question.

Your preview told you that
_____ a. the king is the most important ant in the colony.
_____ b. ants get much done by working together and sharing.
_____ c. all ants do the same work.
_____ d. the queen ant builds rooms.

Turn to the Comprehension Check on page 44 for the right answer.

Now read the story.
Read to find out how ants help each other.

Life In An Ant Colony

This ant colony has many rooms, and each room has a special purpose.

Staying alone can be a nice way to live. Still, most people do better with the company of others. When people live together, they can be of great help to each other. That is why human beings have always lived in groups. Even cave men and women lived in groups in their caves. Some hunted and some cooked. Some acted as guards. By living and working together, they lived through many hard times.

For American Indians, living together has long been a part of their way of life. Indians are free to live where they choose. Yet many Indians still live on reservations. On the reservations they can live much as they would in other places. But they are with other humans who have some of the same needs and problems as they have.

Animals, as well as humans, live and travel in groups. There are many different names for these animal groups. Fish swim in ''schools.'' Wolves run in ''packs.'' We speak of a ''pride'' of lions. One of the most familiar and interesting groups of all, though, is found in the insect world. It is the ''colony'' of ants.

The most important ant in each colony is the queen. Sometimes an ant colony has more than one queen. Queens spend their lives laying eggs. The other ants in the colony are children of the queen. It is the children who do all the work. The children are called ''workers.''

Some workers build the rooms and tunnels of the colony. They burrow through the ground, making the colony home larger and larger. Scratching their way through the soft earth, they build tunnels and rooms that lead to other tunnels and rooms. They burrow this way and that way, always busy. They also carry some of the earth outside, grain by grain, forming a small hill around the open hole. We know this as the familiar ant hill.

The workers build a special room for the queen in the middle of the colony. They build other rooms for the new baby ants that hatch from the queen's eggs. Some workers act as nurses to take care of the babies. Some workers take care of the queen. As the babies grow, they, too, become workers.

Some workers become hunters. They leave the colony each day, searching for food. A piece of garbage carelessly tossed by a human hand can become a feast for the ants. A crumb from a human can be an ant's dinner.

An ant has two stomachs. One stomach is for the food she eats when she is hungry. The other stomach is for the food she saves. Often, a hunter ant will bring back food in this stomach to share with the other ants. She can pass the food from her stomach to the stomach of a hungry ant.

Sometimes a hunter ant will try to bring a large piece of food back to the nest, but will not be able to do it alone. If it is too heavy for her to carry, she will return to the colony for help. One or more ants will go back with her to share the load.

Have you ever seen ants around a garbage pail? Did you wonder how so many of them got there? Sometimes a hunter ant will find food that cannot be brought back to the colony. Then she will return and let the others know about her find. The ants that are able will follow her back to the food.

Sometimes ants "milk" other insects, much as humans milk cows. At an ant's gentle touch, the little insect will let out a sweet, wet drop for the ant to drink.

Some ants act as guards for the ant colony. These ants have larger heads than the other ants. Their heads are too large for the inside work of building and taking care of the queen and babies. Carrying those big heads around, they get tired quickly if they hunt for food. Instead, they spend most of their time near the ant hill, protecting the colony. Sometimes they fight enemy ants.

When the weather becomes really cold, the workers close the ant holes. All the ants crawl into the deepest rooms and settle into a winter sleep. They do not wake again until the weather becomes warm.

Working and sharing together, ants get much done. For their size, it is a wonder that they do it all. Ants do not give up. If one cannot do something alone, others will help. If one is in trouble, others will help. Ants could teach humans a good lesson, if we would pay attention.

Life In An Ant Colony

COMPREHENSION CHECK

Choose the best answer.

1. People have lived in groups
   ____a. only in the past few years.
   ____b. only in this country.
   ____c. for a long, long time.
   ____d. for a short time only.

2. Ants live in
   ____a. a school.
   ____b. a colony.
   ____c. a reservation.
   ____d. a pride.

3. The queen's job is to
   ____a. build rooms.
   ____b. build tunnels.
   ____c. hunt for food.
   ____d. lay eggs.

4. The queen is the most important ant in the colony
   ____a. because she is so pretty.
   ____b. because she has a special room.
   ____c. because she lays all the eggs.
   ____d. because she is a good hunter.

5. The worker ants are
   ____a. friends of the queen.
   ____b. children of the queen.
   ____c. enemies of the queen.
   ____d. food for the queen.

6. The worker ants
   ____a. all do the same job.
   ____b. sleep all summer.
   ____c. lay eggs.
   ____d. do different jobs.

7. Ants have
   ____a. two heads.
   ____b. four eyes.
   ____c. two stomachs.
   ____d. ten legs.

8. The ants with larger heads
   ____a. build the rooms.
   ____b. are the hunters for the colony.
   ____c. milk insects.
   ____d. fight enemy ants.

9. Another name for this story could be
   ____a. "Ants Are Funny."
   ____b. "How to Live Alone and Like It."
   ____c. "The Poor Little Ant."
   ____d. "Group Living."

10. The main idea of the story is
   ____a. too many ants live together.
   ____b. Indians should live on reservations.
   ____c. living things can be of help to each other.
   ____d. it is better to live alone.

Check your answers with the key on page 53.

Idea starter: Why is life in a colony good for ants?

Life In An Ant Colony

VOCABULARY CHECK

Fill in the empty spaces by writing in the correct key word from the box.

burrow	colony	familiar	garbage	human	reservation

What Am I?

1. You do not want to eat me.
   You throw me away.
   But I can be a feast for an ant.

   I am _____ .

2. I am a living thing.
   I am not a wolf, a lion, a fish, or an ant.
   I am like you.

   I am _____ .

3. I am in America.
   I am a place where Indians can live.
   They do not have to live here if they don't
   want to.

   I am a _____ .

4. I am something that living things do.
   I am a word that means "to dig."
   When living things do this, they dig under and
   through the ground.

   My word is _____ .

5. You know me very well.
   As soon as you see me, you remember me.

   That is because I am so _____ .

6. Ants live in me.
   They work together here.
   They help each other here.

   I am a _____ .

Check your answers with the key on page 59.

So You Want To Be An Astronaut!

Learn the Key Words

adjust   (ə just′)
1. to become comfortable with something new
   She had to adjust to her new job.

2. to change something
   He had to adjust the size of his seat belt.

condition   (kən dish′ ən)   a way of being
He was in a weak condition and needed special care.

experience   (eks pir′ ē əns)   something that happened
Her accident was an awful experience.

frontier   (frun tir′)   the nearest part of a new place, which has not been explored before
The pioneer built a house on the frontier.

future   (fü′ chər)   a time that will happen after now
That may happen many years in the future.

program   (prō′ gram)   a plan to be followed
She followed an exercise program to build up her strength.

Preview:

1. Read the title.
2. Look at the picture.
3. Read the first two paragraphs of the story.
4. Then answer the following question.

Your preview told you that
_____ a. there is a new frontier: the West.
_____ b. there is a new frontier: the East.
_____ c. there are no more frontiers.
_____ d. astronauts are much like pioneers.

Turn to the Comprehension Check on page 49 for the right answer.

Now read the story.

Read to find out how astronauts are chosen and trained.

So You Want To Be An Astronaut!

Astronauts travel in space only after they have completed long, hard training.

Many years ago, the American frontier was the place for adventure. People went to that frontier to explore the new country. Years passed, and they were followed by pioneer settlers. The settlers made the West their home. Every experience was a new one for them. They had much to learn about the land. Today, the West is settled. There is some wild country, but it is not as it was before. The American frontier is gone, but there is still a new frontier for us. That frontier is space.

Have you ever thought about being a pioneer? Do you like new experiences? Are you interested in the new frontier? Then you might like to be an astronaut. Astronauts are much like the explorers and pioneers of years ago. But there are some differences.

To begin with, of course, an astronaut travels in space. As with the work of all pioneers, there is much danger in the job. The astronaut tries to learn as much as he can about space. He tries to find ways that we can live in space.

Not everyone can be an astronaut. You have to be chosen to be one. To be an astronaut, you have to be an American. Because of the size of the spaceships, you cannot be taller than six feet. As there is much to know, you would have to go to school for many years before you could be an astronaut.

Even if you met all these

conditions, you still might not be chosen. You would have to prove to a group of doctors that you would be a good person for the space program. You would have to pass their tests.

In one test, you might find yourself in a dark and quiet room. The room would have a chair, a bed, and some food. You would have to be in the room, all alone, for many hours. The doctors would be trying to learn how you would feel under these conditions. They would want to know how you would act under these conditions. They would see how you adjust to darkness, and to being lonely.

The doctors would give you a high mark on this test if you were really clever. You would get a high mark if you spent your time writing something interesting. You would get a high mark if you spent your time working out number problems. You would not get a high mark if you just sat and let your mind wander. You would get a low mark if you could not remember how you had spent your time.

In another test, you might have a box with many lights and buttons. The lights would keep changing. You would have to adjust the buttons to change the lights back. The faster the lights changed, the faster you would have to adjust the buttons. You would get a high mark if you did not give up.

These are two of the tests that have been used in choosing people for the space program. In the future, the tests may be different. But there probably will always be tests, as not everyone can become an astronaut.

If you were chosen to be an astronaut, you would then enter a training program. You might have to train for years before you were ready. Part of the training would be in a special school. You would have to learn many things about space and spaceships. You would go on field trips to parts of the earth that look like parts of the moon. You might also go on field trips to places where people build the machines you would use. You would learn how to use the machines. You would learn how to fix them if they broke down.

You also would be trained in a "pretend" kind of way. You would be put in a room where the conditions had been adjusted to feel like conditions in space. You would learn how to adjust to these conditions. For example, you would learn how to eat and drink while floating in the air.

You would also learn how to stay alive after your spaceship returned to earth. You would learn how to get out of your spaceship in the water. You would also have to learn how to get out under the water, should your spaceship sink.

If you were an astronaut, our future in space might be up to you. It would not be an easy job, but it would be exciting. Think it over.

So You Want To Be An Astronaut!

COMPREHENSION CHECK

Choose the best answer.

1. Today there is
   ____a. no frontier.
   ____b. an American frontier in the West.
   ____c. a new frontier.
   ____d. an old frontier.

2. Astronauts are like the early pioneers because
   ____a. they travel in space.
   ____b. they have an easy job.
   ____c. they are learning about new places.
   ____d. they live in the West.

3. To be an astronaut, you have to
   ____a. be taller than six feet.
   ____b. live in another country.
   ____c. be a sailor.
   ____d. go to school for a long time.

4. The test in the dark, quiet room is given because
   ____a. astronauts write stories about dark places.
   ____b. it is dark and lonely in space.
   ____c. astronauts must do number problems to count their money.
   ____d. some astronauts make too much noise.

5. The box with lights is
   ____a. to make you happy.
   ____b. to make you sad.
   ____c. to help your eyes and hands.
   ____d. to see if you can stay at a difficult job.

6. In the future,
   ____a. the tests may be different.
   ____b. the tests will always be the same.
   ____c. there will never be tests.
   ____d. there will be just one test.

7. If you were chosen to be an astronaut,
   ____a. you could start right away.
   ____b. you could start in two weeks.
   ____c. you would take a train to your job.
   ____d. you would enter a training program.

8. Astronauts sometimes take field trips to
   ____a. places that look like the moon.
   ____b. national parks.
   ____c. the zoo.
   ____d. their home towns.

9. Another name for this story could be
   ____a. "It's Easy to Be an Astronaut."
   ____b. "How One Becomes an Astronaut."
   ____c. "Two Tests for Astronauts."
   ____d. "Why Do You Want to Be an Astronaut?"

10. The main idea of this story is
    ____a. being an astronaut is a lot of fun.
    ____b. being an astronaut is no fun at all.
    ____c. one must work and study hard to become an astronaut.
    ____d. we can all become astronauts if we try.

Check your answers with the key on page 53.

Idea starter: **Why do some people want to become astronauts?**

So You Want To Be An Astronaut!

VOCABULARY CHECK

I. *Complete the story by writing in the correct key words from the box. Some words will be used more than once.*

adjust	condition	experience	frontier	future	program

Grandfather was a pioneer settler in the West. He lived on the American (1) _____ . One winter he had an

(2) _____ he never forgot. It was very, very cold. He found it hard to (3) _____ to the (4) _____ of the weather. There was a snow storm. His cattle wandered away. Some of the cattle fell over a cliff.

Grandfather did not want this to happen in the (5) _____ . He built fences around his land. He thought about the weather for the whole year. Because of his bad (6) _____ with the snow storm, he made a plan to help him be ready for weather changes in the

(7) _____ . He planned when he would fix things on his land. He planned how to take care of his cattle. He followed this

(8) _____ for many years.

II. *Draw a line from the key word to the word (or words) that tell what it means.*

adjust   a way of being

condition   plan

experience   someplace new

frontier   change

future   after now

program   something that happened

Check your answers with the key on page 59.

KEY WORDS
Lessons D-1 — D-10

D-1

business
freedom
government
officer
prison
soldier

D-2

clover
discovery
distance
language
messenger
swarm

D-3

awoke
difficult
disappointment
groan
laughter
wheelbarrow

D-4

anger
attention
dock
fin
leap
wound

D-5

avoid
grateful
interrupt
opinion
racket
scamper

D-6

bracelet
cobbler
creature
graze
stole
unicorn

KEY WORDS
Lessons D-1 — D-10

D-7
court
develop
perfect
position
quarter
realize

D-8
crew
dangerous
hurricane
thankful
voyage
Wednesday

D-9
burrow
colony
familiar
garbage
human
reservation

D-10
adjust
condition
experience
frontier
future
program

COMPREHENSION CHECK ANSWER KEY
Lessons D-1 — D-10

LESSON NUMBER	QUESTION NUMBER										PAGE NUMBER
	1	2	3	4	5	6	7	8	9	10	
D-1	b	a	d	c	b	c	(b)	c	△d	□c	4
D-2	b	c	a	d	d	b	c	(c)	△c	□b	9
D-3	c	a	c	a	d	b	a	(d)	△d	□c	14
D-4	b	c	a	d	(b)	a	b	d	△c	□c	19
D-5	(a)	c	c	b	(b)	a	(d)	b	△c	□d	24
D-6	b	c	a	c	b	d	d	(c)	△d	□a	29
D-7	c	a	b	d	c	b	d	(a)	△c	□d	34
D-8	b	c	a	b	d	a	d	(c)	△b	□d	39
D-9	c	b	d	(c)	b	d	c	d	△d	□c	44
D-10	c	c	d	(b)	d	a	d	a	△b	□c	49

Code: ◯ = Inference

△ = Another Name for the Selection

▢ = Main Idea

NOTES

VOCABULARY CHECK ANSWER KEY
Lessons D-1—D-10

I.   1.   officer
    2.   business
    3.   prison
    4.   soldier
    5.   government
    6.   freedom

I.   1.   language
    2.   swarm
    3.   messenger
    4.   distance
    5.   clover
    6.   discovery

VOCABULARY CHECK ANSWER KEY
Lessons D-1—D-10

D-3   THE OLD MAN WHO DREAMED HIS FORTUNE

I. 1. wheelbarrow
  2. disappointment
  3. groan
  4. awoke
  5. laughter
  6. difficult

D-4   MOBY MAYBE

I. 1. c
  2. b
  3. d
  4. a
  5. c
  6. a

VOCABULARY CHECK ANSWER KEY
Lessons D-1—D-10

I.
1. grateful
2. interrupt
3. avoid
4. racket
5. scamper
6. opinion

I.
1. stole
2. unicorn
3. graze
4. stole
5. bracelet
6. graze
7. creature
8. cobbler

VOCABULARY CHECK ANSWER KEY
Lessons D-1—D-10

I.
1. c
2. b
3. a
4. a
5. d
6. c

I.

II.
1. thankful
2. hurricane
3. crew
4. dangerous
5. voyage
6. Wednesday

VOCABULARY CHECK ANSWER KEY
Lessons D-1—D-10

D-9   LIFE IN AN ANT COLONY   45

I.   1.   garbage
       2.   human
       3.   reservation
       4.   burrow
       5.   familiar
       6.   colony

D-10   SO YOU WANT TO BE AN ASTRONAUT!   50

I.   1.   frontier   *II.*   adjust ———— a way of being
       2.   experience   condition ———— plan
       3.   adjust   experience ———— someplace new
       4.   condition *or* experience   frontier ———— change
       5.   future   future ———— after now
       6.   experience   program ———— something that
       7.   future   happened
       8.   program

NOTES